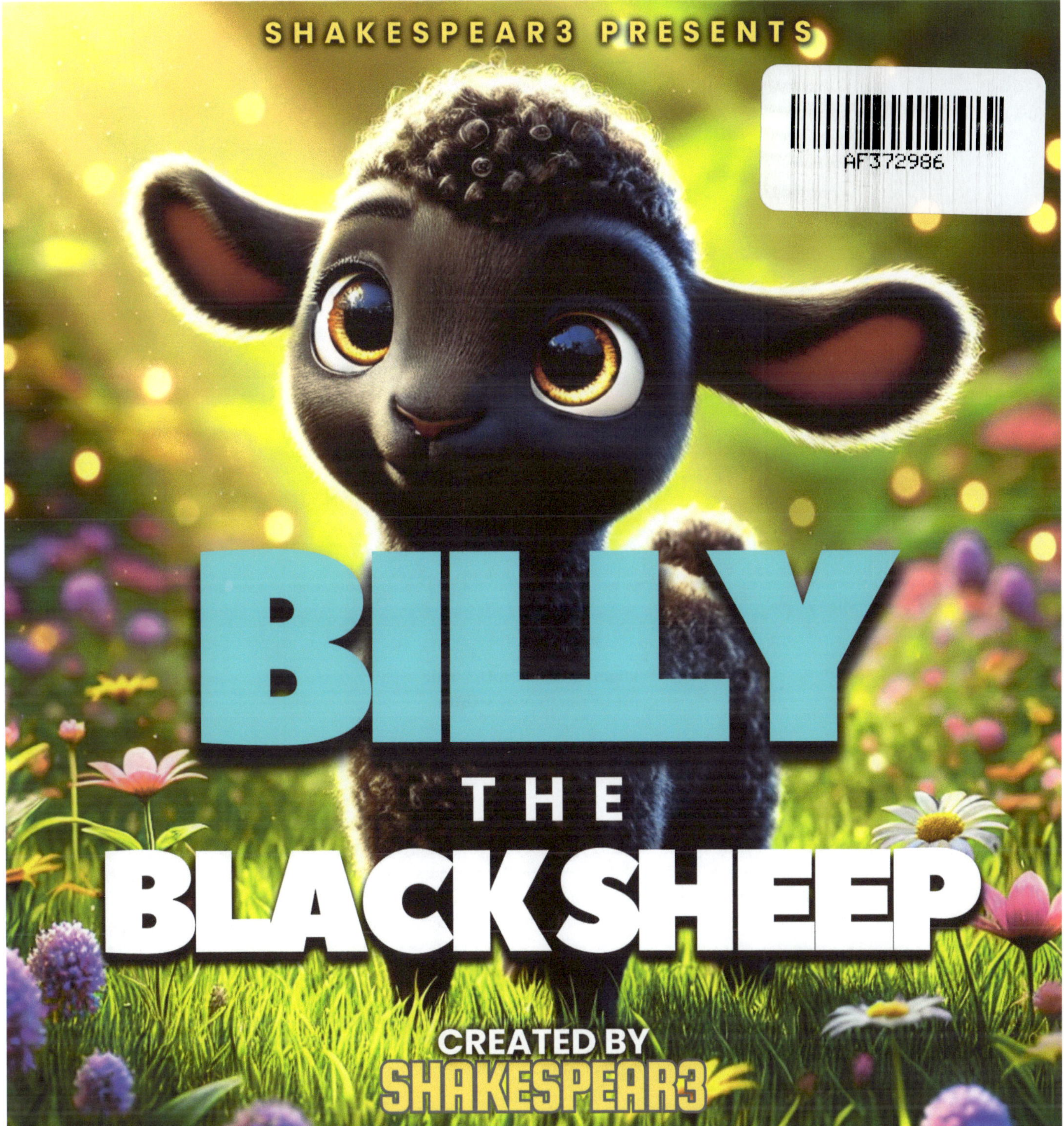

SHAKESPEAR3 PRESENTS
AF372986
BILLY
THE
BLACK SHEEP
CREATED BY
SHAKESPEAR3

Dedication to:

All my children.
Though daddy wasn't always there.
You were always with me in my heart. I hope that
through the great deeds our family will contribute to
humanity. You will be proud, knowing our sacrifices
were not in vain.

In Memory of :
Tammy Lynn Belle

Once upon a time, in a green and sunny meadow, there lived a little lamb named Billy.
But Billy wasn't like the other lambs. While their wool was soft and white, Billy's wool was black as midnight and sparkled like tiny diamonds.

Billy didn't think his wool was special. In fact, he thought it was a curse.

The other lambs would laugh and call him names. Even the big sheep whispered and pointed. Whenever Billy tried to play, the lambs would run away, leaving him all alone.

This made Billy feel very sad. Every day, he would climb to the high hill and cry.

One day, as Billy sat on the hilltop, a soft breeze tickled his wool. When he looked up, he saw a mystical, silver sheep standing beside him.

"Hello, Billy," said the sheep. "My name is Baba."

Billy blinked in surprise. "How do you know my name?"
"Oh, I know all about you," Baba said with a kind smile.
"Why are you so sad?"
"Because no one likes me," Billy said, his voice trembling. "They think I'm ugly because I'm different." I just want to have friends who like me.

"HeHeHe," Baba chuckled gently.
"Oh, Billy, don't you know?
Ugly isn't a real word. It's just short
for 'U Gotta Love Yourself.' And you,
my friend, are the most beautiful
lamb in the whole meadow."

Billy's eyes widened. "Really?"
Imagining in his head that he was an
adorable little sheep prince.

"Really," said Baba. "You just need to look inside your heart and mind. You can be whatever you dream to be. First you believe—and then you'll achieve.
"How do I do that?" Billy asked, tilting his head.

"Next time you climb to your high place," Baba said, "don't cry. Close your eyes and imagine your dreams. See yourself as you truly are." Remember Billy believe and you can achieve.

And with that, Baba faded away like
a magical mist.

The next day, a big storm rolled into the meadow. The sky grew dark, and lightning cracked like fireworks. The wind howled, and all the sheep huddled together, shivering in fear.

But not Billy.

He stood tall and strong, his black wool shining in the stormy light. He ran through the fierce wind, up and up, until he reached the highest hill.

There, at the top of the hill, Billy
closed his eyes. He didn't cry. Instead,
he looked deep inside his heart and
mind.

What he saw was magical.
He saw a world bursting with color, where everything was bright and happy. He saw himself, big and strong.
The sheep who had teased him looked silly, their faces goofy and their wool striped like candy canes & cotton candy!

For the first time in his life, Billy felt pure joy. He smiled—a warm, glowing smile that lit up the stormy sky.

The next morning, the storm was gone. The meadow sparkled with sunlight, but something was different.

Billy was gone.

The other sheep searched high and low, but they couldn't find him. They missed Billy deeply.

His courage and kindness had changed their hearts. From that day on, the sheep learned to celebrate each other's differences.

No matter if a lamb's wool was white, black, or spotted, the herd became one big, loving family.

And sometimes, when the sun set behind the hills, the sheep would look up at the highest peak. They'd see a strong, regal black sheep standing tall, surrounded by his tribe, his black wool shining like diamonds.

They knew it was Billy.

And in their hearts,

Billy the Brave Black Sheep was with them forever.